WORLD:

Hiking and Camping

Paul Mason

A&C Black • London

Produced for A & C Black by
Monkey Puzzle Media Ltd
11 Chanctonbury Road
Hove BN3 6EL, UK

Published by A & C Black, an imprint of
Bloomsbury Publishing Plc
50 Bedford Square
London WC1B 3DP

www.acblack.com
www.bloomsbury.com

First published in paperback 2012
Copyright © 2012 Bloomsbury
Publishing Plc

ISBN 978-1-4081-4036-9

A CIP catalogue record for this book is
available from the British Library.

Editor: Dan Rogers
Design: Mayer Media
Picture research: Lynda Lines

This book is produced using paper that
is made from wood grown in managed,
sustainable forests. It is natural,
renewable and recyclable. The logging
and manufacturing processes conform
to the environmental regulations of the
country of origin.

Printed and bound in China by C&C
Offset Printing Co.

1 3 5 7 9 10 8 6 4 2

Picture acknowledgements
Action Images p. 8 (Axiom/Zuma Press);
Alamy pp. 4 (Chris Cheadle), 6 (Hawaii
Photo Resource), 9 (Ashley Cooper),
10 (SCPhotos), 12 (The National Trust
Photolibrary), 13 (Stuart Forster), 14
(John Warburton-Lee Photography),
18 (Mediacolor's), 22–23 (Jörg Müller),
25 (Photoshot), 26 (Robert Preston),
28 (Alex Ekins), 29 (Peter Raven/
Mark Custance); Corbis pp. 5 (Stefanie
Grewel), 7 (Anthony West), 20 (Whit
Richardson); Florida Trail Association
p. 16 (Robert Coveney); iStockphoto
pp. 15, 27; Paul Mason p. 17; Photolibrary
pp. 1 (Bill Stevenson), 11 (Bill Stevenson),
21 (Bill Stevenson/Superstock), 23 top
(John Warburton-Lee Photography),
24 (Robert Harding Travel/Christopher
Rennie); Wikimedia pp. 18–19, 19 top.
Compass rose artwork on front cover
and inside pages by iStockphoto. Map
artwork by MPM Images.

The front cover shows a hiker by his
campfire in the Chugach State Park,
Alaska, USA (Alamy/Alaska Stock).

SAFETY ADVICE

Don't attempt any of the
activities or techniques
in this book without the
guidance of a qualified
guide or instructor.

CONTENTS

It's a Wild World   4

Na Pali Coast   6

The South Downs Way   8

The John Muir Trail   10

The Lake District   12

The Blue Mountains   14

Kissimmee River Trail   16

Kungsleden   18

Zion National Park   20

The Western Isles   22

The Inca Trail   24

Annapurna Sanctuary   26

Mt Kilimanjaro   28

Glossary   30

Finding Out More   31

Index   32

It's a Wild World

Imagine sleeping in your tent, wrapped up warm and cosy in a sleeping bag. You're surrounded by the sounds of nature: the wind in the trees, or gentle surf on a beach, perhaps. You wake at dawn, unzip the tent and enjoy the sunrise. Hiking and camping can take you there!

THE WORLD OF HIKING AND CAMPING

Hiking and camping gets us away from the world most people live in – the world of cars and concrete, noise and pollution. Just an hour's hike can take you out into nature. You might spot anything from a bear to a tiny dormouse! Camping adds in the fun of an overnight trip.

PASSPORT TO HIKING AND CAMPING

Everything you need to know about hiking and camping is gathered together in this book. Even better, you can find out about some of the best hiking trails and camping spots in the world – though you might need to save up for a while to get to some of them. But hiking and camping don't have to be expensive: basic equipment can be quite cheap and there's certain to be somewhere to visit not far from your home.

What a great place to wake up! A hotel room with a view like that would probably cost you a fortune.

THE SECRET LANGUAGE OF HIKING

Hiking does not require lots of equipment. The most important things are good places to walk and good friends to walk with.

terrain type of ground, e.g. rocky, steep, flat, etc.
thermal to do with heat. Thermal underwear helps keep you warm.

Technical: Hiking checklist

Before going on a hike, it's worth checking that you are taking the right clothing and equipment with you. Exactly what to take depends on the **terrain**, the temperature and how far you are going, but here are a few basics:

Warm-weather/summer hiking:

• Comfortable walking boots or shoes and comfortable socks (special hiking ones have padded toes and heels).

• Loose or stretchy clothing.

• A warm layer and a waterproof top.

• Plenty of water, and food if you are going to be walking for over an hour.

• A hat and sunscreen.

• A map, and a mobile phone with emergency numbers.

For cold weather, take everything you would take in summer, plus:

• A warm hat and gloves.

• An extra warm layer, and possibly **thermal** underwear.

• Always wear long trousers, never shorts.

• In snowy conditions, wear sunglasses to protect your eyes.

Na Pali Coast

The Hawaiian island of Kauai would be a great place to head to for your first-ever hike. The temperature rarely drops below 16° Centigrade (61° Fahrenheit) even at night, and in summer anything more than a light shower of rain is unusual. One of the most beautiful parts of the island is the Na Pali coast.

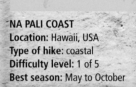

NA PALI COAST
Location: Hawaii, USA
Type of hike: coastal
Difficulty level: 1 of 5
Best season: May to October

HIKING THE NA PALI COAST

The Na Pali coast is made up of *pali*, or cliffs, broken up by narrow valleys and a few beautiful beaches. Hikers can follow the Kalalau Trail, an ancient path originally built by native Hawaiians to reach their terraced fields. A good one-day walk on the trail goes between the beaches at Ke'e and Hanikapi'ai, and back.

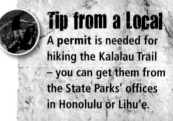

Tip from a Local
A **permit** is needed for hiking the Kalalau Trail – you can get them from the State Parks' offices in Honolulu or Lihu'e.

Stunning views along the north-western coast of Kauai, Hawaii.

THE SECRET LANGUAGE OF HIKING

permit piece of paper giving permission
purifying making clean

ESSENTIAL INFORMATION

Whatever time of year, the air temperature is almost never uncomfortably high or low in Hawaii. In winter, though, heavy rainfall can be uncomfortable and make the trail slippery.

Clothing: Travel light, but always take rain gear, even in summer, in case of a shower.

Other equipment: Mosquito repellent will definitely be useful in the evenings.

Hazards: Be careful of the ocean at Hanikapi'ai, as the surf and currents here can be very strong.

If you like Na Pali...

... you could also try:
• Abel Tasman Coast Track, New Zealand
• Lycian (pronounced "lick-ee-an") Way, Turkey

Clothes for a week? Check. Skis and ski boots? Check. Teddy bear? But of course! She may well have the kitchen sink in that pack, too.

Deciding what to take on a hike can be tricky. If you take too much, the extra weight will spoil your day. But so could searching in your bag for a rain jacket, only to find you left it at home! Here are a few tips:

• You will warm up after a few minutes of walking. If you are the perfect temperature when you set off, you will probably soon be too hot. Maybe you could lose a layer?

• Never scrimp on water or food. Experts recommend people drink at least 2–3 litres (3.5–5.3 pints) of water a day, more when doing hard exercise or in hot weather. When going away for days, water-**purifying** tablets may come in handy.

The South Downs Way

The South Downs is home to some classic English countryside. The Way starts in the ancient city of Winchester, crosses the rolling countryside and farmland of Hampshire and Sussex, and ends at the white, chalky cliffs near Eastbourne on the south coast.

HIKING THE SOUTH DOWNS WAY

The entire route is 160 kilometres (100 miles) long – much too far for a single day's hiking. Most people hike along a shorter section of the route. With plenty of train stations, bus stops and teashops, it's easy to plan a day's hike anywhere between Winchester and Eastbourne.

THE SOUTH DOWNS
Location: Hampshire/Sussex, England
Type of hike: coastal
Difficulty level: 1.5 of 5
Best season: May to September

The South Downs Way is one of Britain's most popular long-distance trails. It passes through some of the most beautiful countryside in Southern England.

Tip from a Local

The Devil's Dyke is beside the South Downs Way – it's a steep-sided valley said to have been dug by the Devil, as part of his plan to drown a nearby village.

If you like the South Downs Way...

... you could also try:
- The Loire Valley Trail, France
- Tahoe Rim Trail, California/Nevada, USA

THE SECRET LANGUAGE OF HIKING

tops high ground at the top of a hill or mountain

escape finish a hike early because something has gone wrong

ESSENTIAL INFORMATION

The best chance of good weather is in summer, but this is England – it can rain at any time of year. In winter, snowfall occasionally makes the Downs look more like Lapland.

Clothing: In summer, light clothing and shoes are fine; in winter, it can be very cold and windy up on the exposed **tops**.

Other equipment: A map covering the section you are walking will make an **escape** easier, if the weather turns bad.

SKILL
Following way-markers

Where there's a choice of routes, it's not always easy to find your way even if there are trail signs. It's always a good idea to carry a map of the area with you as a backup.

Many official hiking routes are marked out so that they are easier to follow. Following a way-marked trail is a great way to get into hiking. It makes it much harder to get lost!

• Follow the direction markers carefully: if you miss one, you may have to retrace your steps. Sometimes the signs show more than one route: always double check you are following the right one, in the right direction!

• Take a map of the route with you as a backup. (Usually these can either be downloaded from the Internet, collected at a visitor centre or bought from a shop.)

The John Muir Trail

The John Muir Trail is regularly voted one of the top ten hiking trails anywhere in the world. It winds its way through some of North America's most beautiful scenery. The trail starts in the Yosemite National Park and finishes 246 kilometres (153 miles) later at Mt Witney.

THE JOHN MUIR TRAIL
Location: California, USA
Type of hike: mixed
Difficulty level: 2 of 5
Best season: June to September

Setting up camp for the night at a high spot on the John Muir Trail.

THE SECRET LANGUAGE OF HIKING

bear canister airtight container for food, which stops its smell from reaching hungry bears' nostrils!

Tip from a Local

John Muir (1838–1914) was a Scottish-American who campaigned for the protection of the USA's wilderness areas.

If you like the John Muir Trail...

... you could also try:
- The Overland Track, Tasmania, Australia
- Alta Via (High Way) number 1, Italy

A hiker high above the Yosemite Valley takes in the view.

Hiking the John Muir Trail

Hiking the whole trail at once takes most people up to a month. It is easy, though, to do sections of the trail that take as little as a day. From Yosemite Valley, the trail passes through the Ansel Adams Wilderness, Sequoia National Park and Kings Canyon National Park.

Weather and equipment

The trail is probably best for improvers in summer, when lightweight gear should be suitable for day-long walks. At other times of year the weather and temperature can change rapidly, meaning rain gear and warm clothes may be needed. Anyone sleeping overnight on the trail will need **bear canisters** – so that bears do not come prowling into your camp at night!

The Lake District

The wild beauty of the Lake District has inspired famous poets such as William Wordsworth, and artists such as John Ruskin. When you hike or camp in the Lake District, you are probably visiting the most famous countryside in Britain – and maybe even the world.

THE LAKE DISTRICT
Location: Cumbria, England
Type of hike: mixed
Difficulty level: 2 of 5
Best season: May, June and September

HIKING IN THE LAKE DISTRICT

Many hikers come to **the Lakes** to climb the high mountains, or "fells". These include Scafell Pike, the highest peak in England, and Helvellyn. The classic route to Helvellyn runs along Striding Edge, a narrow path along a sharp **arête**. There are also many beautiful walks along the sides of the lakes.

If you don't like the weather in the Lake District, wait half an hour. Up here in the mountains, it changes very quickly.

Tip from a Local

Bassenthwaite Lake is the only official "lake" in the Lake District – all the rest are known as either "mere" or "water".

Technical: Tents and sleeping bags

If you are camping out, you will only get a good night's sleep if your tent keeps you dry and your sleeping bag keeps you warm.

• Tents with an inner and outer layer are best. The outer layer keeps rain out. The inner will have a groundsheet sewn in, to keep you off wet ground (and stop ants crawling into your sleeping bag!).

• Sleeping bags are rated for warmth, usually by season. A 1- or 2-season bag is really for summer only, 3-season is good for everything except cold weather, and 4-season is for winter.

• Never pitch your tent in a hollow or on low ground – if it rains, that will be the first place to flood! If you get cold at night, pulling on a hat will warm you up.

Always try to find a level spot for your tent – otherwise everyone ends up rolling to one side during the night!

 ## THE SECRET LANGUAGE OF HIKING

the Lakes short for the Lake District
arête ridge of rock that is steep-sided and narrow at the top

If you like the Lake District...

… you could also try:
• The Lakes Area of New Hampshire, USA
• Mziki Hiking Trail, South Africa

ESSENTIAL INFORMATION

Whatever time of year you visit, there's a good chance it will rain. The warmest months are June to September – but during the August school holidays, the Lakes can be so crowded that it takes the fun out of visiting.

Clothing: ALWAYS take wet-weather gear and a warm top, even in summer. At any other time of year, cold-weather kit will be needed.

Other equipment: A map of the area, and a mobile phone with the mountain-rescue number stored in its memory.

Hazards: Sudden storms, ice or snow during winter.

The Blue Mountains

For years after Europeans first arrived in Australia, the Blue Mountains were a barrier they were unable to cross. They did finally break through, and today the area is criss-crossed by some amazing trails (as well as roads and railway lines).

THE BLUE MOUNTAINS
Location: New South Wales, Australia
Type of hike: mixed
Difficulty level: 2.5 of 5
Best season: all year round

Tip from a Local

Leave details of your route and what time you expect to get back with a responsible adult – they can raise the alarm if you don't show up!

Hiking through the thick forests of the Blue Mountains, it's easy to imagine a velociraptor leaping out of a bush at you!

HIKING THE BLUE MOUNTAINS

The Blue Mountains has a fantastic variety of trails. In one hike, you can find yourself gazing out from a high **escarpment** and working your way down a steep rock face. Then you could be picking your way along a fern-filled gully that wouldn't be out of place in a dinosaur movie.

THE SECRET LANGUAGE OF HIKING

escarpment inland place where high ground ends in a cliff

ESSENTAIL INFORMATION

Hiking is possible all year round in the Blue Mountains. In summer (January to March) it can be extremely hot, and many people think spring and autumn are the best times to visit.

Clothing: Warm-weather gear is usually enough, plus a warm top and a rain jacket.

Other equipment: Take plenty of water, and a map and compass.

Hazards: Australia is full of natural hazards, including poisonous snakes and spiders – watch out!

SKILL
Map reading

Binoculars or a monocular are sometimes useful for identifying landmarks shown on a map.

Every year, people get into trouble in the Blue Mountains because they have got lost. The area is very wild, and if you lose the established trails it becomes very hard to find your way. Good map reading is an essential skill.

• The best way to use a map is never to lose track of your position on it. Trace the route you're planning to take on the map before you leave on a hike.

• Every time the trail passes a landmark, such as a lake, or the path forks, or you go up or down a steep slope, check the map to see if you are still going the right way.

• If you are unsure, retrace your steps until you find a landmark you know is right, then start again from there.

If you like the Blue Mountains...

..., you could also try:
• The Atlas Mountains, Morocco
• Dartmoor, England

Kissimmee River Trail

Part of the fun of hiking is spotting the kind of wildlife you just don't see in town. This walk through a remote part of Florida offers lots of chances to spot some amazing animals, including cranes, deer, wild turkeys, wild hogs, hawks, alligators and eagles.

KISSIMMEE RIVER TRAIL
Location: Florida, USA
Type of hike: flat
Difficulty level: 2.5 of 5
Best season: January to April

Tip from a Local
There are ten campsites along the trail, so it is a good choice for an overnight stop or two.

Along parts of the Kissimmee River Trail, trees provide some welcome shade.

HIKING THE KISSIMMEE RIVER NATIONAL SCENIC TRAIL
Unsurprisingly, this trail runs alongside the Kissimmee River. It is 53.4 kilometres (33.2 miles) long, and is part of the larger Florida Trail, which runs right through the state. The stretch along the Kissimmee River is a relatively easy walk across flat land. Hikers pass through swampland, pine flatlands and oak **hammocks**.

If you like the Kissimmee River Trail...

... you could also try:
- Derwent River Walk, England
- Lake Waikaremoana Track, New Zealand

ESSENTIAL INFORMATION

The trail can be very wet and is best hiked in the dry season, between January and April.

Clothing: Light clothing only, as the daytime temperature is usually warm or hot all year round.

Other equipment: Bring plenty of water, insect repellent, sunscreen and a sun hat.

Hazards: In theory, poisonous snakes, and alligators – though you would be very unlucky to meet either. You'll find the biting insects much more annoying.

THE SECRET LANGUAGE OF HIKING

hammock area of raised ground in a wetland

points of the compass north, south, east and west

equator imaginary line around the middle of the Earth

SKILL
Finding your way without a map

This is an easy way to work out the **points of the compass**. It takes about two hours, either side of midday.

1. Push a stick about 30 centimetres (12 inches) long into the ground, pointing straight upwards.

2. Every 10 minutes, mark the tip of the stick's shadow with a pebble.

3. Keep doing this until you find yourself putting pebbles further from the stick, because the shadow is getting longer.

4. The line from the base of the stick to the nearest pebble will be pointing roughly north-south. South of the **equator**, north is at the stick end. North of the equator, north is at the pebble end.

Finding direction in the wilderness. A line from the stick to the second stone from the left runs roughly south-north.

Kungsleden

Lapland lies in the far north of Sweden – so far north that in summer, it never gets dark. Crossing this wild territory is the Kungsleden, or "King's Trail". For 425 kilometres (264 miles), the route crosses some of northern Sweden's most breathtaking landscapes (that's breathtaking in both senses of the word!).

KUNGSLEDEN
Location: Lapland, Sweden
Type of hike: mixed
Difficulty level: 3 of 5
Best season: May to July

MOUNTAIN LANDSCAPES

From the north, the trail heads south through the Kebnekaise mountain range. These are Sweden's highest mountains. On a clear day, you can see almost a tenth of Sweden from the top of the Kebnekaise. Then the trail runs south again, through more mountains, heading for the "Golden Gate".

THE GOLDEN GATE

The Golden Gate lies between the villages of Ammarnäs and Hemavan.

It is a group of islands connected by five suspension bridges and two plank bridges. The scenery here makes a great change from the mountains further north.

STOPPING PLACES

All along the Kungsleden are mountain huts and hostels, where you can unroll your sleeping bag at night and buy food and water. It is easy to do short sections of the trail for two or three days, getting dropped off at one hut and being picked up from another.

A hiker makes his way carefully over one of the suspension bridges along the Kungsleden.

Tip from a Local

Tip from a Local

During spring, it is possible to follow the Kungsleden on **telemark** skis – it's a popular trip at Easter.

Even when snow covers the ground, a few hardy cross-country skiers enjoy following the route.

Not a good moment to remember you left a tap on at home! The Kungsleden crosses some of northern Europe's most remote wilderness.

If you like the Kungsleden…

… you could also try:
• The Appalachian Trail, Eastern USA
• The West Coast Trail, Canada

THE SECRET LANGUAGE OF HIKING

telemark skis that can travel uphill as well as down and along flat ground

Zion National Park

Zion National Park has something for every kind of hiker. The lower-level paths offer the chance for an easy morning or afternoon's walk. Some are wheelchair accessible. The higher, more remote tracks will test the skills of even the most experienced hiker.

ZION NATIONAL PARK
Location: Utah, USA
Type of hike: mixed
Difficulty level: 3 of 5
Best season: May, June, September and October

Over the centuries, water has carved the canyons into wonderful, eerie shapes.

If you like Zion...

... you could also try:
- **Supramonte Mountains, Sardinia, Italy**
- **Kings Canyon National Park, California, USA**

Tip from a Local
Always take plenty of water into Zion – on most trails, none is available.

Hiking Zion

Zion is famous for its **canyon** hikes, which follow deep, river-cut canyons through the **sandstone**. The most popular of these is The Narrows, a tough, 26-kilometre (16-mile) hike following the Virgin River. The trail passes alongside canyon walls that are 600 metres (1969 feet) high, and in places only 10 metres (33 feet) apart. For the complete experience, camp out at one of the 12 camping spots along the canyon.

Essential information

It is possible to hike in Zion all year, but during winter the higher areas can be cold, icy and snowy. The lower areas are much safer and, for most people, more enjoyable.

Clothing: In summer it is important to protect yourself from the sun and from overheating. Cover up using light, loose clothing and a sun hat.

Other equipment: Definitely put insect repellent and plenty of water in your pack.

Hazards: The canyons can flood during or after heavy rain. If the water gets mucky or starts to rise, find higher ground at least 2 metres (6.6 feet) above the river and wait it out.

THE SECRET LANGUAGE OF HIKING

canyon steep-sided, narrow river valley

sandstone soft, light-coloured type of rock

SKILL
Cooking safely out of doors

You can easily cook a simple meal on a basic, lightweight gas stove like this one.

Fires are only allowed in some of Zion's official campgrounds. Elsewhere, the risk of fire means only camping stoves may be used. Even then, it is important to be careful.

1. Set up your stove on a hard, level surface such as a flat rock. Have it as far as possible from anything flammable.

2. If your stove uses liquid fuel, pour it in without spilling any, seal the fuel bottle and put it at least a metre (3.3 feet) away.

3. When lighting the stove, make sure any matches you use have been completely put out, by dunking them in water.

4. When you have finished cooking, make sure the stove is fully out. Do not leave it unattended until it is cool to the touch.

The Western Isles

In the Western Isles, steep-sided mountains rise up from the sea, begging you to climb them and enjoy the view. The white beaches of the islands offer a change of scene, where you can look for otters and seabirds – or just enjoy your packed lunch on the sand!

THE WESTERN ISLES
Location: Scotland
Type of hike: mixed
Difficulty level: 3 of 5
Best season: May, June and September

HIKING AND CAMPING THE WESTERN ISLES

The Western Isles pack a huge variety of landscapes into a small area. Hiking is made even more attractive by the Scottish "right to roam". This law says that ordinary people are allowed to walk on almost all open land, even if it is privately owned. You are also allowed to camp, in small groups, for two or three nights.

The dramatic, wave-broken coasts of the Western Isles are a hiking paradise (so long as you don't mind a bit of wet weather).

THE SECRET LANGUAGE OF HIKING

day pack small backpack for carrying a day's equipment

scramble hike up a steep slope using both hands and feet

Tip from a Local

For a taste of the Western Isles, visit the island of Arran – it's sometimes known as "Scotland in miniature".

If you like the Western Isles...

... you could also try:
- Vancouver Island, Canada
- Brijuni Islands, Croatia

ESSENTIAL INFORMATION

In May, June and September, you have the best chance of good weather without the dreaded "midges" – tiny biting insects that can become a real pain in summer.

Clothing: In Scotland, there's *always* the chance of rain and cold weather. Even on the warmest day, pack accordingly.

Other equipment: In summer, some people walk in hats with "midge curtains" of fine mesh hanging from the brim.

Hazards: Midges! Also, in winter, high winds and heavy rain can cause real danger.

SKILL
Ascending and descending rough ground

On some hikes, a bit of near-climbing (called scrambling) is needed.

The steep-sided slopes of the Scottish mountains can be hard work and very tiring to walk up – and even down. A few hiking tips can help make things easier.

• Never carry more than you need up a mountain. If you are taking a side trip from a long hike, find somewhere to leave your heavy pack and just take a **day pack**.

• When walking uphill or downhill, take lots of small steps instead of a few big ones. It is far less tiring over the course of a long walk.

• Never walk above a pace at which you can carry on talking to your friends, as your body will then start to use up energy very quickly.

• On steep slopes, use your hands to help you **scramble** upwards.

The Inca Trail

High up in Peru's Andes Mountains lies the Inca city of Machu Picchu. It was discovered only recently, having been hidden from the world for hundreds of years. Today, hikers can follow an ancient trail that winds up to Machu Picchu through the mountains.

Don't look down! Avoid the trail to Machu Picchu if you're nervous about heights or steep drops!

THE INCA TRAIL
Location: Andes Mountains, Peru
Type of hike: mountainous
Difficulty level: 3.5 of 5
Best season: May to September

Tip from a Local

Watch out for orchids on the trail – you will spot lots of beautiful examples of these rare flowers.

If you like the Inca Trail...

... you could also try:
- The Lares Trail, Peru
- Hadrian's Wall Path, England

Hiking the Inca Trail

There are two main versions of the trail. The first takes four days, the second seven. Both feature breathtaking views of snow-capped mountains and Inca ruins. Having reached Machu Picchu, most hikers walk to the town of Aguas Calientes, which is 6 kilometres (3.7 miles) away. From there, they can catch a train or bus to their next destination.

Essential information

The trail is driest between April and October. In the wet season, between January and March, it can be waterlogged and miserable.

Clothing: Travel as light as possible, but be prepared for very hot days and very cold nights.

Other equipment: It's very important to have a warm sleeping bag.

Hazards: Cold at night; heat during the day; **altitude sickness**.

THE SECRET LANGUAGE OF HIKING

altitude sickness headache, sickness and confusion caused by high altitude. Unless the sufferer climbs down, it can lead to death.

pack out pack up and take away with you

Always pack out your rubbish – if you leave yours behind, other people will probably decide it's OK to leave theirs, too.

Avoiding trail damage

Hikers in large numbers damage the very landscape they have come to enjoy. The Inca Trail has to close every February, so that the damage caused by thousands of hikers can be repaired. Here are some ways to minimize this damage:

• Stick to the trail. When people wander off the trail it creates new paths, wearing away the vegetation and soil.

• Only camp where camping is allowed, and move your tent after a night or two so that the grass underneath it is not damaged.

• **Pack out** what you bring into wilderness areas. Never leave behind rubbish of any kind, especially not plastics or metals that will hang around for years.

Annapurna Sanctuary

ANNAPURNA SANCTUARY
Location: Nepal
Type of hike: mountainous
Difficulty level: 4 of 5
Best season: February to May
and September to December

Almost every hiker dreams of one day visiting the Himalayas. It offers the chance to trek through the world's highest mountains, visiting villages you can only reach on foot. The dramatic scenery and friendly Nepali people make this a hiking paradise.

LAND OF THE GODS
Annapurna Sanctuary is a high **plateau** surrounded by the Annapurna Mountains. The only way in or out of the Sanctuary is a narrow pass between two peaks. Inside is a land held sacred by the Gurung people, who until 100 years ago were the only humans to know the area. They believed the Sanctuary was home to many gods – including Shiva, chief of all the gods.

Tip from a Local
The trek to Annapurna Sanctuary is a **"teahouse trek"** – you stay in teahouses, rather than camping, so there's no need to bring a tent.

Flags with prayers printed on them, on the trail to Annapurna Sanctuary. Buddhists believe that as the flags flap in the wind, the prayers are carried to heaven.

The view from a teahouse balcony – imagine waking up and opening your door to this! Teahouses offer hikers food and a place to stay so that they don't need to carry tents.

HIKING TO THE SANCTUARY

The hike usually takes between eight and ten days, starting from the small town of Nayapul. It follows paths and tracks that wind along the mountainsides, dropping into steep valleys before rising up again – it can feel as though you haven't moved very far after a whole day's walking! Temperatures vary from very cold at night to boiling hot at midday – a variety of clothes will *definitely* be needed.

If you like Annapurna Sanctuary...

... you could also try:
• Tongariro Circuit, New Zealand
• Los Glaciares National Park, Argentina

THE SECRET LANGUAGE OF HIKING

plateau flat area of high ground

teahouse mixture of café and hostel found in the Himalayas

Mt Kilimanjaro

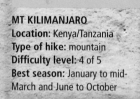

MT KILIMANJARO
Location: Kenya/Tanzania
Type of hike: mountain
Difficulty level: 4 of 5
Best season: January to mid-March and June to October

Kilimanjaro is not only the highest mountain in Africa but also one of the biggest volcanoes on Earth. Fortunately, it is 360 000 years since the volcano's last major eruption – so the chances of being toasted alive by a river of molten lava are slim!

It might be in Africa, but it still gets snowy and cold at the summit of Mt Kilimanjaro.

Tip from a Local

If potatoes are served for dinner on the first night, don't miss out – they will all be cooked then because they're so heavy to carry!

Information: The Seven Summits

Kilimanjaro is one of the "Seven Summits". These are the highest mountains on each of the Earth's seven continents.

• Kilimanjaro is the only one of the Seven Summits that can be climbed without specialist climbing skills. Mt Kosciusko in Australia is an easy hike, and used to be included in the list.

It has now been replaced by Carstensz Pyramid in Indonesia, which is over twice as high.

• The Vinson Massif would be an easy climb – if only it wasn't the highest mountain in Antarctica! The freezing temperatures and high winds make it an impossible challenge without specialist equipment.

CLIMBING KILIMANJARO

Kilimanjaro is 5895 metres (19 341 feet) above sea level, and it is possible to hike to the summit in five to seven days. You do need to be fit and experienced, though! There are six main routes to the summit, starting from either Tanzania or Kenya. The easiest routes are Rongai (on which people sleep in tents) and Marangu (with hut-based shelter).

If you like Mt Kilimanjaro...

... you could also try:
- Mt Kosciusko, Australia
- Ben Nevis, Scotland

Like Kilimanjaro, many mountains have a choice of routes up and down. Experienced hikers always pick the route that will suit the slowest, least-fit member of their group, so that everyone will be able to hike together.

ESSENTIAL INFORMATION

Kilimanjaro is best climbed during its two dry seasons. Of these, January to March is quieter but colder; June to October is busier but warmer.

Clothing: Shorts and a T-shirt are usually fine during daytime. But in the evening and at night the temperature drops and it can be very cold (there is always snow at the summit).

Other equipment: You'll need a sleeping bag, water bottles and purification tablets, sunscreen and sunglasses.

Hazards: Altitude sickness, which kills several people each year on Kilimanjaro.

THE SECRET LANGUAGE OF HIKING

summit highest point

Glossary

WORDS FROM THE SECRET LANGUAGE FEATURES

altitude sickness headache, sickness and confusion caused by high altitude. Unless the sufferer climbs down, it can lead to death.

arête ridge of rock that is steep-sided and narrow at the top

bear canister airtight container for food, which stops its smell from reaching hungry bears' nostrils!

canyon steep-sided, narrow river valley

day pack small backpack for carrying a day's equipment

equator imaginary line around the middle of the Earth

escape finish a hike early because something has gone wrong

escarpment inland place where high ground ends in a cliff

hammock area of raised ground in a wetland

pack out pack up and take away with you

permit piece of paper giving permission

plateau flat area of high ground

points of the compass north, south, east and west

purifying making clean

sandstone soft, light-coloured type of rock

scramble hike up a steep slope using both hands and feet

summit highest point

teahouse mixture of café and hostel found in the Himalayas

telemark skis that can travel uphill, as well as down and along flat ground

terrain type of ground, e.g. rocky, steep, flat, etc.

the Lakes short for the Lake District

thermal to do with heat. Thermal underwear helps keep you warm.

tops areas of high ground at the top of a hill or mountain

OTHER WORDS HIKERS AND CAMPERS USE

bivvy short for "bivouac", meaning an overnight stay with little or no shelter

cairn cone of rocks piled up to mark the route of a trail

camel up drink as much water as possible

GPS Global Positioning System, a way of finding your route using a hand-held computer and satellite signals

hiker midnight 9 p.m. (because most hikers are so tired that they're usually fast asleep by then…)

potable describes water that it is safe to drink (so, "non-potable" means do NOT drink it!)

switchback tight turn in a trail as it goes up or down a steep slope

through hiker someone who is walking the entire length of a long-distance trail

weight weenie someone who is determined to hike with the lightest possible pack

Finding Out More

THE INTERNET

www.ramblers.org.uk
This site has information about hiking in Britain, including the country's National Trails and Long Distance Routes.

www.yha.org.uk
The YHA (Youth Hostel Association) has inexpensive accommodation available around the country, usually in great hiking areas. If you don't want to stay in a tent, this is a good alternative.

www.ukcampsite.co.uk
Put the name of a town into this site's search engine, and it will tell you about nearby campsites; or you can search by clicking on a map.

BOOKS

INFORMATION BOOKS

Hiking and Camping Paul Mason (Macmillan Library, 2008) and *Camping and Hiking* Neil Champion (Wayland, 2010)
Both books contain basic information for young readers about hiking and camping, including useful equipment and techniques.

Be Prepared: Hiking and Backpacking Karen Berger (DK Publishing, 2008)
Longer and with more detailed coverage, this book is aimed at older, teenage readers and adults, but confident younger readers will also find it useful.

OTHER BOOKS

The Complete Idiot's Guide To Camping and Hiking Michael Mouland (Alpha Books, 1999)
Does exactly what it says on the cover: introduces basic information to people who know nothing about hiking and camping. Plenty of useful info for experienced hikers, too.

MAGAZINES

Most hiking and outdoor magazines carry a mixture of articles on equipment, personalities, contests and travel. They all have websites you can locate by searching by name.

TGO (short for "The Great Outdoors"), *Trail* and *Country Walking*
These British magazines are focused mainly on British and European hiking.

Outside
This US-based magazine carries high-quality travel articles, features and equipment reviews.

Index

Abel Tasman Coast Track, New Zealand 7
Aguas Calientes, Peru 25
Alta Via number 1, Italy 11
altitude sickness 25, 29
Annapurna Mountains 26
Annapurna Sanctuary, Nepal 26–27
Ansel Adams Wilderness, USA 11
Appalachian Trail, USA 19
Atlas Mountains, Morocco 15

bear canisters 10, 11
Ben Nevis, Scotland 29
Blue Mountains, Australia 14–15
Brijuni Islands, Croatia 23

clothing 5, 7, 9, 11, 13, 15, 17, 21, 23, 25, 27, 29
compass 15, 17
cooking 21

Dartmoor, England 15
Derwent River Walk, England 17
Devil's Dyke, England 8
direction finding 17

equipment 5, 7, 9, 11, 13, 15, 17, 21, 22, 23, 25, 29

Hadrian's Wall Path, England 24
Helvellyn, England 12

Inca Trail, Peru 24–25
insect repellent 7, 17, 21

John Muir Trail, USA 10–11

Kalalau Trail, Hawaii, USA 6
Kebnekaise Mountains, Sweden 18
Kings Canyon National Park, USA 11, 20
Kissimmee River Trail, USA 16–17
Kungsleden, Sweden 18–19

Lake District, England 12–13
Lake Waikaremoana Track, New Zealand 17
Lakes Area, USA 13
Lares Trail, Peru 24
Loire Valley Trail, France 9
Los Glaciares National Park, Argentina 27
Lycian Way, Turkey 7

Machu Picchu, Peru 24, 25
map reading 15
maps 5, 9, 13, 15
Mt Kilimanjaro, Kenya/ Tanzania 28–29
Mt Kosciusko, Australia 28, 29
Muir, John 11
Mziki Hiking Trail, South Africa 13

Na Pali Coast, Hawaii, USA 6–7

Overland Track, Australia 11

"right to roam" 22

Scafell Pike, England 12
Sequoia National Park, USA 11
Seven Summits 28
sleeping bags 4, 13, 18, 25, 29
South Downs, England 8
South Downs Way, England 8–9
Striding Edge, England 12
sunscreen 5, 17, 29
Supramonte Mountains, Italy 20

Tahoe Rim Trail, USA 9
teahouses 26, 27
tents 4, 13, 25, 26, 27, 29
Tongariro Circuit, New Zealand 27

Vancouver Island, Canada 23

water 5, 7, 15, 17, 20, 21, 29
water purifying tablets 7, 29
way-markers 9
weather 5, 9, 11, 12, 13, 15, 17, 22, 23
West Coast Trail, Canada 19
Western Isles, Scotland 22–23

Yosemite National Park, USA 10

Zion National Park, USA 20–21